BLUFF YOUR WAY IN PHILOSOPHY

JIM HANKINSON

RAVETTE BOOKS

Published by Ravette Books Limited
P.O. Box 296
Horsham
West Sussex RH13 8FH
Tel & Fax: (01403) 711443

First printed 1985
Reprinted 1987, 1989, 1991, 1992, 1994

Series Editor – Anne Tauté

Cover design – Jim Wire
Printing & binding – Cox & Wyman Ltd.
Production – Oval Projects Ltd.

The Bluffer's Guides ® is a
Registered Trademark.

The Bluffer's Guides ® series is based
on an original idea by Peter Wolfe.

An Oval Project
for Ravette Books Ltd.

CONTENTS

INTRODUCTION

What Philosophy Is

This is something you should always contrive to avoid explaining. But you might like to get two things straight at the start.

Firstly, philosophy isn't a subject – it's an activity. Consequently one doesn't study it: one does it. This is how philosophers, at least those in the Anglo-Saxon tradition (which for some obscure historical reason seems to include the Finns), tend to put it. And secondly, philosophy is largely a matter of conceptual analysis – or thinking about thinking. For the moment, let's stick to basics.

This is something most philosophers find temperamentally impossible, but there's no reason why you should follow their example. Philosophy seems, to the casual visitor taking a swift look round it, bewilderingly complex. Not least among its difficulties is the fact that philosophers, with a few honourable exceptions, find it quite impossible to speak a language comprehensible to the ordinary person, such as English. A philosopher wanting even to refer to the Ordinary Person (a species with which he is unlikely to have had first-hand acquaintance, although he may have heard travellers' tales about them) will call him 'the man on the Clapham Omnibus', unaware, apparently, both that no-one uses the word 'omnibus' any more except to refer to large collections of detective fiction, and that Clapham is no longer an ideal example of drab inner-London mediocrity.

Your task, therefore, is to get at least a tenuous grip on the more arcane reaches of the technical vocabulary which is deployed in such a baffling way by the contemporary philosopher. Don't worry. Linguistic competence, as the later Wittgenstein would have said (not to be confused, of course, with the earlier Wittgenstein, who wouldn't) is a matter of getting words in the right order. You won't actually have to understand what, if anything, most of it means.

LIVES OF THE PHILOSOPHERS

Philosophy is a subject (sorry, an activity) with a history: and because it makes so little progress, if indeed it makes any at all, its history is consequently more important than that of other fields. The successful bluffer must be armed with a working knowledge of this history if he or she is to make a real success of charlatanry.

For the purposes of this book, we will confine ourselves almost exclusively to Western philosophy, that tradition begun in Greece in the 7th century B.C. There is a good reason for this. Philosophy in the Western tradition is a very different type of project from that of the Orient. In a later section we will give some advice on how to be suitably dismissive about such matters as Meditation, Buddhism, Indian Religion, People with Shaven Heads in Grubby Yellow Robes, and similar social menaces.

Accordingly, this section contains some more or less interesting facts about some more or less famous philosophers, of both a biographical and a philosophical nature, in roughly chronological order.

The first Greek philosophers are known generally, if misleadingly as the *Presocratics*. Misleadingly, as not all of them came before **Socrates**, and in any case they formed no coherent school: many of them in fact didn't even form coherent individuals.

No-one knows why philosophy started when it did: ambitious bluffers of a Marxist bent could try to account for it in terms of an inexorable dialectic of historical forces, but we wouldn't recommend it. A notable feature of many of them is their attempt to reduce the material constituents of the Universe to one or more basic Stuffs, such as Earth, Air, Fire, Sardines, Old Cloth Caps, etc.

Thales of Miletus (c. 620-550 B.C.) was the first recognised philosopher. There may have been others before him, but no-one knew who they were. He is remembered chiefly for two claims:

1) Everything is made of Water; and
2) Magnets have souls.

Not an auspicious start, you might think.

Anaximander (c. 610-550) thought everything was made of the Boundary and the Unlimited, a conception which has a certain spurious appeal, until you realise that it is quite meaningless.

Anaximenes (c. 570-510), struck out boldly in a new, if arbitrary, direction, saying that everything was really made of Air, a view perhaps more plausible in Greece than, for instance, Motherwell.

Heraclitus (c. 540-490) disagreed, thinking rather it was Fire everything was made of. He also went a stage further by claiming that everything was in a state of flux and identical with its opposite, adding that you couldn't step into the same river twice, and that there was no difference between Up and Down, both of which show that he'd never been on a walking holiday in the Peak District. It is sometimes worth referring, in passing (always the best way to refer to things in philosophy), to 'Heraclitus's Metaphysic', meaning the flux, as long as there's no danger of your having to explain yourself. Heraclitus was greatly admired by **Hegel** (*q.v.*), which perhaps says more about Hegel than about Heraclitus.

Pythagoras (c. 570-10), as every schoolchild knows, invented the right-angle triangle; in fact he went further, believing that everything was made of numbers. He also believed in an extreme form of reincarnation, holding that a wide variety of improbable things, including shrubs and beans, had souls, which made his diet problematic, and was indirectly responsible for his bizarre death (*q.v.*).

Empedocles (c. 500-430), a notable 5th century Sicilian

political wheeler-dealer, physician, and nut-case (see Deaths for details) thought everything was made of Earth, Air, Fire and Water, held together, or broken down, by Love and Strife, each taking it in turns to get the upper hand in a cycle of eternal recurrence, thus making the cosmos mirror, on a large scale, the average suburban marriage.

Then we get the *Eleatics*, **Parmenides** (520-430) and **Melissus** (480-420), who went further still. Instead of contending that everything was in fact made of one substance, they held that there was in reality only one Thing, large, spherical, infinite, motionless, changeless. All appearance of variety, motion, separateness of objects, etc., is an Illusion. This extraordinarily counter-intuitive theory (sometimes known as **Monism**, from the Greek word 'mono', meaning an antiquated recording system) proved surprisingly popular, no doubt because it accorded with people's experience of such institutions as British Rail and the Gas Board.

Their successor, **Zeno** (500-440), advanced a series of paradoxical arguments to the effect that nothing can move. Achilles and the Tortoise is still discussed, as is the Arrow: he argued that it couldn't possibly move, which, if true, would have been good news for St. Sebastian. The arguments turn largely on the question of whether Space and Time are infinitely divisible, or whether one or both is made up of indivisible *quanta:* mention this to give Zeno a modern-sounding air; if called upon to back it up, change the subject.

Last among the Presocratics come the *Atomists*, **Democritus** (c. 450-360) and **Leucippus** (450-390). They are sometimes held responsible for anticipating modern atomic theory. This is quite false, and one scores useful points by saying so, for the simple reason that the crucial thing about Democritean atoms is that they can't be split, whereas the crucial thing about modern ones is that they can. You might also point out that Democritus didn't like sex, though whether for theoretical reasons, or whether because of some unfortunate personal mishap, isn't known.

So much for the Presocratics: now for the man himself, **Socrates** (469-399). Socrates didn't write anything: we rely on Plato for information about him, and it is a vexed question how much Plato reproduced Socrates' own views, and how far he simply used his name. Don't get embroiled in it: a useful ploy here is to say, with a certain lofty contempt, that philosophical content is what matters, not its historical provenance.

Plato (427-347) believed that ordinary everyday objects like tables and chairs are merely poor 'phenomenal' copies of perfect Originals that are laid up in Heaven to be appreciated by the intellect, the so-called Forms. There are also Forms of abstract items such as Truth, Beauty, Goodness, Love, Overdrafts, etc. This got Plato into some difficulties: for if everything we see, feel, touch, etc., has its existence in the virtue of some Perfectly Good Form, there must be Perfectly Good Forms of Perfectly Awful Things. Plato himself mentions hair, mud and filth; we can think of better examples, such as Nodding Dogs and Spanish package-tour souvenirs.

Plato seems to be grossly overrated as a philosopher: the following is a typical Platonic argument, from Book 2 of the *Republic*, if you don't believe it:
1) Anything that distinguishes between things on the grounds of knowledge (as opposed, presumably, to mere prejudice) is a philosopher;
2) Guard-dogs distinguish between things (in this case visitors) according to whether or not they know them (this is a truth well known to postmen); ergo
3) All guard-dogs are philosophers.

Try that one out for size sometime.

Another useful line with Plato is to argue either:

1) that he was a feminist;
2) that he wasn't.

Both claims can be supported, and each may turn out to be handy (at different times, of course). The evidence for 1) is that, in Book 3 of the *Republic*, he says that women should not be discriminated against in matters of employment solely because they are women. In favour of 2) is the fact that immediately afterwards he remarks that since women are so much less talented than men by nature, this 'liberalisation' will make hardly any difference anyway.

After Plato comes **Aristotle** (382-322), sometimes known as the Stagirite, which is not something you find dangling in pot-holes, but a native of Stagira in Macedonia. He was a pupil of Plato's, and expected to succeed him as head of the Academy. Accordingly, he was somewhat put out when **Speusippus** (no need to know anything about him) got the job, and went off in a huff to found his own school, the Lyceum – not to be confused with the ballroom of the same name.

Aristotle was quite disgustingly brilliant. He made contributions to Logic (in fact he invented it), Philosophy of Science (he invented that too), Biological Taxonomy (yes, he invented that one as well), Ethics, Political Philosophy, Semantics, Aesthetics, Theory of Rhetoric, Cosmology, Meteorology, Dynamics, Hydrostatics, Theory of Mathematics, and Home Economics. It is rarely advisable to say anything uncomplimentary about him, but the confident bluffer might venture to regret the excessively Teleological bias of his Biology, or remark that, for all that his logical theory was a remarkable achievement, nonetheless it has of course been superseded by modern developments owed to Frege and Russell (*q.v.*). But take care with this, and never use it in conversation with a mathematician, even quite a young one. A fairly safe line to take is to be moderately disparaging about the more ludicrous aspects of Aristotle's Biology, such as the following argument concerning the structure of the snake's genitalia:

'Snakes have no penis, because they have no legs; and they have no testicles, because they are so long.'

(*De Generatione Animalium*)

He offers no argument to support the first contention, except one supposes it would drag along the ground in a painful manner; but the second derives from his reproductive theory. For Aristotle, semen is not produced in the testicles, but in the spinal column (the testicles function apparently as a sort of rest-area for the travelling sperm); furthermore, cold semen is infertile, and the further it has to travel, the colder it gets (hence the well-known fact, he remarks, that men with long penises are infertile). So, given that snakes are so long, if the semen stopped off anywhere on the way, snakes would be infertile; but they aren't; therefore they have no testicles. This splendid argument is an example of Excessive Teleology, or explanation in terms of goals and purposes, in this instance really a matter of getting everything back to front.

After Aristotle, philosophy gets increasingly fragmented. Several rival schools were formed to complement, and argue the toss with, the already existing Academy and Lyceum. The major new arrivals at the beginning of the 3rd century B.C. are the *Stoics*, the *Epicureans* and the *Sceptics*.

The *Stoics* believed, perversely, in an all-embracing Divine Providence, in spite of all evidence to the contrary, such as the occurrence of natural disasters, the prevalence of injustices, the existence of haemorrhoids. **Chrysippus**, perhaps the most prominent, and certainly the most verbose of the Stoics, argued that bedbugs had been created by a Benevolent Provider to stop people from over-sleeping. The Stoics also made important developments in logical theory, which enabled them to formulate types of argument that had eluded Aristotle. But you shouldn't worry too much about that.

The *Epicureans*, named after their founder, **Epicurus** (342-270) held that pleasure was the End, and that this consisted in the satisfaction of desires, which was a good start. But then they had to foul things up by arguing that this didn't mean a lot of pleasure was a good thing: rather, one should limit the number of desires one had, so you didn't get left with as many unsatisfied ones, a project which makes for a miserably dull life (and would, if carried through, entail a radical restructuring of the fantasy-life of the average adolescent). This is a logical point of view, if not a lot of fun, and of course radically opposed to that view of philosophy which sees it essentially as a pursuit of the Ineffable and Unattainable: Mystic Union with the Creator, Total Empathy with the Cosmos, an Affair with Catherine Deneuve. Thus:

'By pleasure we mean the absence of mental and physical pain. It isn't a matter of boozing, orgiastic parties, or indulgence in women, small boys, or fish.'
(from the *Letter to Menoeceus*)

We don't know where he got the idea of fish from, but assure you it's there in the text. The other important feature of Epicureanism was their version of Atomic Theory, which was like Democritus's, except that, in order to preserve Free Will, Epicureans held that every now and again the atoms swerved unpredictably, causing collisions, rather like reckless city motorcyclists. They also held that although the gods existed, they didn't give a damn about human affairs, as they'd got better things to do.

The other major school of the period, the *Sceptics*, didn't believe anything. Their founder, **Pyrrho of Elis** (c. 360-270) didn't write any books (presumably because he didn't believe anyone would read them if he did), although later Sceptics, somewhat pointlessly one would have thought, did so, notably **Timon** who wrote a book of lampoons called the *Silli*, **Aenesidemus** and **Sextus Empiricus.** Their main line of argument was that no sensory report was trustworthy, though it might be pleasurable, and consequently one couldn't be sure of anything. Indeed, one couldn't be sure of the fact that one couldn't be sure of anything. To support this view, they adduced versions of the Argument from Illusion, which Descartes was later to employ.

It is said that Pyrrho's scepticism was such that friends repeatedly had to stop him from walking off cliffs, under passing chariots, into rivers, which must have been a full-time job, although they seem to have been pretty good at it, as he lived to a ripe old age. He is said to have visited the Indian Gymnosophists, or 'naked philosophers', so-called from their habit of conducting nude seminars. He once got so irritated by repeated public questioning that he stripped off his clothes (perhaps under the influence of the Gymnosophists) leaped into the illusory River Alphaeus, and swam powerfully away, a tactic the hard-pressed bluffer might well consider emulating.

There were some further minor schools struggling to get in on the act, most notably the *Cynics,* who were masters of the snide remark, and hell to have round for dinner. One of their number, **Crates**, was known as 'The Gate-crasher' because of his habit of bursting into people's houses and insulting them. The most famous Cynic was **Diogenes**, who lived in a barrel to avoid paying rates, and once memorably, if rashly, told Alexander the Great to get out of his light. He also scandalised people by eating, making love, and masturbating in public places, as and when the mood took him

It can be useful to pretend an affection for the Cynics: they didn't give a tinker's cuss, if indeed they knew any, for what anyone else thought of them and are consequently either models of the Philosophic Temperament, or boorish oafs, depending on your point of view. It doesn't matter what it is, but make sure to have one.

Philosophy pottered on in the Greco-Roman world under the unpredictable patronage of the Roman emperors whose attitudes to philosophers varied considerably. Marcus Aurelius, for instance, was one himself; Nero, on the other hand, killed them. The influence of Christianity began to be felt in this period and philosophy suffered as a result.

Augustine, who for some bizarre reason became a saint in spite of his prodigal sex-life and his famous prayer to God to 'make me chaste: but not just yet', had some interesting ideas. He anticipated Descartes' Cogito (I think, therefore I am; *always* refer to it as the 'Cogito'), and developed a theory of time according to which God stood outside the temporal stream of events (being Eternal and Unchangeable, he pretty well had to), which means that the Almighty never knows what time anything is, rather like the average railway official.

There were also the *Neoplatonists*, some of whom were Christian and some of whom weren't, whose names all seem to begin with a 'P'. The Christians among them were dedicated to showing that Plato had really been a Christian, an idea requiring a startling, not to say implausible, temporal reorganisation. Neoplatonists tended to talk of Abstract Things with Capital Letters, such as the One and Being, in a manner no-one could understand. This is not a fault confined to them: Heidegger did it as well, but then he was a German, and you have to expect that sort of thing from the Germans. You will come across people who profess an admiration for this group: don't hesitate to dismiss them out of hand, especially **Plotinus**, **Porphyry** and **Proclus**, though you may allow, grudgingly, that the latter had some interesting ideas about Causes.

After that came the Dark Ages, and the flame of philosophy, as verbose historians are inclined to put it, was kept alive in the Arab world, and in monasteries that were either too remote or too poverty-stricken to be worth sacking. Philosophy, insofar as it existed in Europe at all, took a depressingly theological turn, centering on disputes as to whether God was One person in Three or Three people in One, the exact nature of the Substance of the Holy Spirit, and how many angels can dance on top of a Goblin Teasmade (in the unlikely event of their actually wanting to).

It is perhaps worth drawing attention to Cordoba in Southern Spain, which, under the Arab occupation, was the home of the greatest Jewish philosopher, **Maimonides**, and the greatest Arab philosopher, **Averroes**. Some will hold that Avicenna, not Averroes, was the greatest Arab philosopher – but don't give way (dogmatism pays). For several hundred years Jew, Arab and Christian managed to live together there. Religious intolerance, though perennial, has not been an invariable fact of life.

Philosophy in Europe began to revive in the 11th century with **Anselm**, another of the philosophical saints, who is famous for having invented the misleadingly-named Ontological Argument for the existence of God, which is remarkable for its implausibility its longevity, and the difficulty one has in refuting it. It goes like this: think of something greater than which nothing can exist; but existence itself is a property that makes something better.* So if this greatest thing (i.e. God) doesn't exist, there would be a yet greater thing imaginable, namely an existent God, having all the same properties as the other one with the added bonus of existence. But we can conceive this. So God must exist. Anselm himself tells us that God sent the argument to him in a vision shortly after breakfast on the 13th of July 1087, when he was having a bit of a sticky time with his faith. It is thus the only major argument in philosophical history whose discovery can be precisely dated. Unless of course Anselm was telling fibs.

The next important philosophical saint was **Thomas Aquinas** (1225-74), who was largely responsible for the re-introduction of Aristotle into the Western tradition. (He had been politely ignored for several centuries by scholars who didn't like to admit they couldn't understand Greek.) St. Thomas is also the only philosopher officially recognised by the Catholic Church. He is notable for propounding the Five Ways of proving the existence of God – he hadn't been much impressed with Anselm. You don't need to know what they are, but you could try pointing out that there isn't any significant difference between the first three Ways, so Aquinas was over-playing his hand.

He is also the author of two interesting arguments against incest. Firstly, it would make family life even more hellishly complex than it is already; and secondly, incest between siblings should be forbidden, because if the love proper to husband and wife were joined to that

*This contention, implausible when applied to halitosis and small children becomes more persuasive if the entity in question is good in all other respects.

17

appropriate between brother and sister the resulting bond would be so powerful as to result in unnaturally frequent sexual intercourse. It is unfortunate that St. Thomas does not define this last intriguing concept. One might also doubt whether he had any brothers or sisters.

As for the rest of the Mediaeval Schoolmen, as they are known from their pedagogic predilection for intense pedantry, most of the important ones seem to have been Franciscans. You should steer clear of them, at least in any detail. You might recall that **Duns Scotus** (1270-1308) was in fact Irish, and was in addition, according to Gerard Manley Hopkins, 'Of reality the rarest-veined unraveller', whatever that means. Another name worth dropping is that of **William of Ockham** (c. 1290-1349), by common consent the greatest of the Mediaeval logicians, best known for 'Ockham's Razor' with which he put an end to centuries of rather hairy philosophy. The Razor is usually quoted in the form: 'Entities Should not be Multiplied beyond Necessity', or better in Latin: 'Entia non sunt multiplicanda praeter necessitatem' (i.e. Cut the Crap). Bluffer's score extra points for remarking that this formulation is not, in fact, to be found anywhere in Ockham's phenomenally logorrhoeic *oeuvre*.

The modern age of philosophy effectively starts with the discovery, in the Renaissance, of **Greek Scepticism**; it was translated by Lorenzo Valla, and employed by Michel de Montaigne. After ascending from Valla to Montaigne, Sceptical Epistemology formed the basis from which Descartes was to rebuild a positive philosophy.

René Descartes, (1596-1650), as almost every First-year philosophy student's essay will tell you, was the Father of Modern Philosophy. Descartes was in many ways a highly engaging character: he had enormous difficulty

18

getting up in the morning, and he invented the Cogito (remember, *always* call it that) while hiding in a stove in Bavaria in 1620 to avoid military service. He never married, but had an illegitimate daughter. It is advisable to memorise Descartes' famous philosophical slogan in at least three languages, as very little mileage can be got out of it in English. Descartes himself published it in both Latin and French: 'Cogito, ergo sum'; 'Je pense, donc je suis' (the version from *Discours sur la Méthode*, which is less well-known than the Latin *Meditations*, and consequently better material for the bluffer). Advanced bluffers can amuse themselves by supplying versions in German, Serbo-Croat, Urdu, etc. Descartes came to the conclusion that this at least was certain, after systematically trying to doubt everything else, starting with comparatively simple things, like oranges, cheese, the real numbers, and gradually working up to really tough ones like God and his landlady.

He discovered he could doubt the existence of everything except the reality of his own thoughts. (He was even a bit doubtful about his own body, and with good reason, if contemporary portraits are anything to go by.) From this unshakeable certainty he proceeded to 're-build a metaphysical bridge' (use this phrase: it sounds good) back into ordinary reality, by way of a proof of the existence of God (quite how needn't concern us: it's enough to know that he did it), thus, in the end, leaving things pretty much the way he'd found them. But then philosophy's like that, as Wittgenstein was to point out. You may legitimately wonder whether it was worth the bother: but on no account let on.

From this point on, philosophy begins to show signs of splitting into two traditions, British and Continental. This sort of remark enrages the French and the Germans, who, not unreasonably, like to think of their individual traditions as being separate – so it comes in handy when talking to them.

The British tend to be lumped together as *Empiricists*, which, as the name suggests, means that they built up their systems from the basis of what could be felt, observed, experienced. The important figures sound like a racial joke: there was an Englishman (Locke), an Irishman (Berkeley) and a Scotsman (Hume). Jokers will be disappointed to discover that, stereotypes notwithstanding, Berkeley was very clever, and Hume very generous.

But we start with **John Locke** (1632-1704) who thought that objects had two sorts of attributes:

1. Primary Qualities such as Extension, Solidity, Number, which are held to be inseparable from and inherent in the objects themselves, and
2. Secondary Qualities, such as Colour, Taste, Smell, which seem to be in the objects, but are in fact in the percipient. (Anyone who has recently passed a field of freshly-spread horse-manure may be disposed to doubt this.)

Quite what one is to do with such attributes as Extreme Nastiness, which seems to be both widespread and objective, no-one is sure: but possibly he would hold that Ugliness, like Beauty, is in the eye of the beholder, which means that there's hope for all of us.

Locke also thought that we had no Innate Ideas (thus the infant mind is a *tabula rasa,* clean slate: as indeed many adult minds appear to be), and that all our knowledge of the external world was derived either directly from experience, or indirectly by extrapolating from it. This gave him some trouble in accounting for highly abstract concepts like Number, Infinity and Edible Fast Food. He held interesting views on the problem of

Personal Identity: How do I differentiate myself from Other Minds? What is the Content of the Continuity of my Personality? Am I the same Person who married my wife five years ago? If so, is there anything I can do about it? etc. contending that not all Men were Persons, for to be a Person requires a certain level of intelligent self-consciousness, and not all Persons were Men. His reason for believing this last rested squarely on his credulous acceptance of a Latin American traveller's account of meeting an intelligent, Portuguese-speaking macaw in Rio de Janeiro.

George Berkeley (1685-1753), in spite of the disadvantages of being both Irish and a Bishop, was more radical. He held that things only exist if perceived ('Esse est percipi': try to remember that), and his reason for believing this extraordinary idea which he seemed to think was simply common sense, was that it is impossible to think of something's being unperceived, for in the very act of trying to think of it as unperceived, you are, by thinking of it, perceiving it.

Berkeley's philosophy had a great vogue, and had the virtue of greatly irritating Dr. Johnson, who claimed to have refuted it by kicking a stone – a peculiarly unphilosophical form of refutation which completely missed Berkeley's point. People who subscribe to such views are called **Idealists** (see Glossary). Like most things in philosophy, they come in more or less lunatic forms; G. E. Moore once remarked that Idealists only believe trains have wheels when they are in stations, as they can't see them when they're on board. It also follows, interestingly, that people don't have bodies except when they're naked, a fact which, if true, would render much everyday speculation pointless.

The natural successor to views of this sort is a kind of Scepticism: and this is where **Hume** (1711-76) comes in.

Hume published his first book, the *Treatise of Human Nature*, in 1739, and was somewhat miffed when no-one took any notice of it. Undeterred, however, he simply rewrote it and issued it under another title (*Enquiry Into Human Understanding*), and people immediately sat up and took notice.

The general view is that the *Enquiry* is much inferior to the *Treatise*: you might try opposing this view (the *Enquiry* has the virtue of being much shorter, for one thing). Among the things it's useful to know about Hume is that he developed an original account of causes, according to which cause and effect are simply the names we give to events or items that have repeatedly been observed to go along with one another: 'Constant Conjunction'. Try pointing out that Hume's three formulations of this principle in the *Enquiry* are not equivalent: one makes causes *necessary* conditions for their effects; the second makes them *sufficient* conditions; the third seems to be ambiguous; and you might note that this principle cannot differentiate between causes and collateral effects. Hume also thought that Free Will and Determinism could be made compatible: politely doubt this probable truth.

Meanwhile, back on the Continent, we should take account of such individuals as **Spinoza** (1634-77), a Jewish lens-grinder from Amsterdam. He was much admired (though not, apparently, by his contemporaries, who first publicly cursed him, then, when that didn't work, tried to have him assassinated) for his Ethical System, which he set out like a set of formal deductions in geometry. Unsurprisingly, given his method, he was a strong Determinist and believed in an unshakeable Logical Necessity.

The best line with Spinoza is to balance admiration for the man with a faint sense of disappointment that he should have employed a system so unsuitable to the subject-matter of ethics. Ethics, one may say apothegmatically (as indeed did Aristotle), is not capable of exhibition in a formal, axiomatised system.

Leibniz (1646-1716) is popularly known as the caricature Pangloss in Voltaire's *Candide*, the optimistic twerp who thinks that everything is for the best in the best of all possible worlds, which is palpable nonsense. However, Leibniz only wrote things like that to comfort monarchs. You'd have thought they were comfortable enough as it was. Leibniz also wrote extensively on Logical and Metaphysical matters, but these speculations were not published in his lifetime, because they weren't very comforting to monarchs. In the unlikely event of his name coming up, reflect sadly on the difference between the quality of Leibniz's private thought and the poverty of his public pronouncements.

Space prevents us from saying much about the French philosophers of the 18th century, whose leading lights were **Voltaire, Rousseau** and **Diderot**. They are remarkable for all having been arrested or exiled, or both. It is becoming fashionable to extol Diderot's originality, good sense, humanity, and fine erotic prose at the expense of the others, and he is worth cultivating if only because little of what he wrote, apart from *La Réligieuse*, The Nun, is readily available in English. Try dropping *Le Reve de d'Alembert* or *Jacques Le Fataliste* into the conversation – and don't forget to mention that he wrote porn for a living.

The **Marquis de Sade** is good value, partly as an example of an extravagantly deviant aristocratic nutter, partly for his brand of state-of-nature philosophy gone mad: his motto might have been 'if it feels good, do it'. It did, he did, and he was locked up for it. You could mention *Philosophie dans le Boudoir*, an extraordinary mixture of socio-biological political and moral philosophy and imaginatively-choreographed sado-masochistic sex. You could wonder tentatively whether his philosophy has been taken seriously enough (it has: but you needn't mention that).

Which brings us on to the 19th century Germans. Our advice is: steer well clear of them. All you need to know about their fore-runner **Kant** can be found in another section (see Ethics). All anyone knows about **Hegel** could be written on the back of a post-card, and even then would be unintelligible. He had, in an advanced form, that talent common to solicitors, computer enthusiasts and German philosophers, of making the basically simple fantastically complex.

He first used the word 'dialectic' to mean the interplay of opposing historical forces, and is thus important in the pre-history of Marxism. Apart from that German philosophical terminology can be most impressive when properly used (see the Glossary). Much the same goes for **Schopenhauer**.

Nietzsche (1844-1900) was something of an odd-ball, and is thus ideal for cocktail-party remarks. Contemporary opinion brackets him with Wagner as a proto-fascist; he was certainly anti-semitic, but then so was virtually everyone else in 19th-century Prussia. He was of the opinion that God was dead or at the very least taking time off, and he hated women fanatically, though it is doubtful if he ever actually met one.

He also advanced a doctrine of Eternal Recurrence, according to which everything happens over and over again in exactly the same way. He professed to find this comforting, but it commits us to an eternity of repetitious tedium, or, if each recurrence is *precisely* similar to all others so none contains memories of any of the others, it makes no difference. Nietzsche went definitively mad in

1888 (some would say he had done so a great deal earlier), and began to write books with headings like *Why I am so Clever*, and *Why I write such Wonderful Books*.

Among the non-Germans of the 19th century, you should mention **Kierkegaard**, if only to show the fact that you know how to pronounce it: 'Keerkergore'.

The most notable French philosopher of the period was **Henri Bergson**. He was a Vitalist, believing that what distinguished animate from inanimate matter was the presence in the former of some mysterious *Élan Vital*, or Life Force, a mysterious and undefined power which for some reason deserts the human body during adolescence. He also, notably, managed to write a long book about laughter that didn't contain a single good joke.

Which brings us to the Americans.

The distinctive American contribution to philosophy at this time was Pragmatism, which is not, as it is in politics, another name for a shabby and self-serving rejection of any principle, but rather the belief that truth and falsity are not absolute but matters of convention, or in a phrase beloved of some modern philosophers, 'Up for grabs'. On reflection, perhaps it does have something in common with politics. This view was held by **William James** and **John Dewey**. If you're going to use these names, don't forget that James was the brother of Henry James, the novelist.

That brings us to the end of the historical section of this enquiry: 20th century philosophers will be treated in a later section (with a bit more care, as many of them are still alive, and thus able to sue).

DEATHS OF THE PHILOSOPHERS

So much for the lives of the philosophers. According to the Epicureans death is nothing to us – but in spite of their opinion, we include the following list of bizarre philosophical deaths, for the sake of completeness.

There are two traditions about **Empedocles'** death. According to one he died of a broken leg; but the other has it that he jumped into the crater of Mount Etna in order to prove that he was a god. How this was supposed to constitute such a proof is not recorded.

Heraclitus, however, contracted dropsy as a result of living off grass and plants on a mountainside in a fit of misanthropy. On being told by doctors that his condition was incurable he undertook his own treatment prescribing that he be first covered from head to foot in manure, and then left out of doors (or perhaps it was just that no-one would have him indoors). According to the historian Diogenes Laertius, 'he was unable to tear the dung off, and, being unrecognisable thus, was devoured by dogs'. Perhaps they wouldn't have done it if they'd known who he was.

Don't mention **Socrates'** death from hemlock in an Athenian jail, as everyone knows about it anyway; but if you are unfortunate enough to have anyone mention it to you, try pointing out that the description of his death in Plato's *Phaedo* is entirely inconsistent with the known effects of hemlock: so someone was lying.

Pythagoras was a victim of his own extreme vegetarianism. Being pursued by several dissatisfied customers, he came to a field of beans, and rather than trample the beans down, he stayed where he was and was killed.

Crinis the Stoic (a school famed for its imperturbability and indifference to worldly fears) died of fright at the squeaking of a mouse. Stoic philosophy never really got over it.

Chrysippus the Stoic, on the other hand, died laughing at one of his own appalling jokes. An old woman's donkey, so the story goes, once ate a large collection of his figs, whereupon he offered the woman his wine-skin, saying: "Better give him a draught of this wine to wash them down with." Then he fell about laughing. Then he died. With a sense of humour like that, one may be forgiven for thinking it a good thing that none of his 700 books survives.

Diogenes is supposed to have died in one of three ways.

1) By not bothering to breathe.
2) From severe indigestion as a result of eating raw octopus.
3) From being bitten on the foot while dividing a raw octopus among his dogs.

After the ancient period, the quality of philosophical deaths falls off considerably, although it is perhaps worth recording that **Aquinas** died on the lavatory as had **Epicurus** before him. **Francis Bacon** died as a result of pneumonia caught while trying to freeze a chicken in the snow on Hampstead Heath. He is probably the only man ever to die from researching into convenience foods, as opposed to dying from actually eating them.

And finally, it was **René Descartes'** misfortune to die of getting up too early in the mornings. Inveigled to the court of Queen Christina of Sweden, he discovered to his horror that she wanted daily tuition, and the only time she could spare was five in the morning. The strain killed him.

THE BASIC QUESTIONS
OF PHILOSOPHY

Your early appreciation of Philosophy must include **Ontology**, which is the study of What There Is, and **Epistemology** which is the study of how we come to know about it. These words can be used in a variety of ways: the student bluffer is advised to stick to a few basic rules to avoid getting into difficulties; the more advanced can make up his or her own.

Epistemology is often linked with the names of individual philosophers, as in 'Plato's epistemology' or 'Kant's epistemology' although one should be very careful about committing oneself in regard to **Kant**, or indeed any other German philosopher.

Ontology is less frequently ascribed to individuals, so don't risk it, unless you're confident that the person you're talking to is more ignorant than you are. In philosophy, this is generally a safe assumption, but be warned: mistakes can be made, and they can prove costly. Ontologies, however, can be more or less rich: in simple terms, the richer the ontology, the more things there are supposed to be.

Quine (Willard van Orman Quine: refer to him as 'Quine', or, if very sure of yourself, 'van Quine'), once observed that all the important questions of philosophy were asked regularly by four year-old children. They are:

1. "What is there?" (ontology);
2. "How do you know?" (epistemology);
3. "Why should I?" (which might be construed as a question in ethics).

Children don't really get on to Metaphysics (*q.v.*) which is probably a good thing. But the most common and irritating juvenile question of them all, "Why?", is the Basic Question of Philosophy.

Levels and Meta-levels

'Meta' is a word, or rather a prefix, that is absolutely essential to the ambitious bluffer. Its use originates with the invention of **Metaphysics** by Aristotle. The literal meaning of 'meta' in Greek is 'with' or 'after', and Aristotle's 'Metaphysics' were thus the things that came after the 'Physics'. It is sometimes imagined that they were so called because they contained truths at a deeper, more arcane, more fundamental level than those of the 'Physics'. This is completely false.

The truth is that in the standard early edition of Aristotle (done by one Andronicus of Rhodes), they came out in the volumes immediately subsequent to those which contained the 'Physics'. As a result of that historical accident, combined with the fact that no-one could come up with any suitable alternative name for the ragbag of logic, theology, epistemology and mathematics that constitutes Aristotle's 'Metaphysics', the term 'meta' has come to signify any study at a deeper level than the study it prefixes.

So, if one does meta-mathematics, and our advice is not to, one studies not the theorems and proofs of maths itself, but the basis for accepting them, and the **Formal Structure** they exemplify. Meta-ethics, similarly, is not the study of what we ought to do, but the study of the nature of the theories that tell us what we ought to do. It will be clear that, properly deployed, 'meta' is a tool of devastating conversational force.

A meta-language is a language in which you discuss

the structure of another language, known as the object language. You might try remarking that the object language is often contained in the meta-language, but never vice versa: don't bother about what that means. So, the last clause, in which we discussed meta-language, was in fact an example of meta-meta-language; and *that* last sentence... well, you get the general idea. There is thus the opportunity of an **Infinite Regress**, the philosophical equivalent of banging your head against a brick wall. **Alfred Tarski**, a logician of the inter-war years when all logicians seemed to be Polish (though not of course vice versa), actually held that only by positing a theoretically infinite hierarchy of languages could we fully explicate (a good word) the notion of truth as it functions in ordinary language. The reasons for this are extremely complex and difficult, and can only be mastered after years of study, so say so.

Easy to link with Tarski, although equally difficult, (some would say impossible) to understand, is the American philosopher **Donald Davidson**, who started off as a theoretical psychologist, but found it really much too easy, and became a philosopher instead. He adapted and expanded Tarski's programme in an attempt to supply philosophy and natural languages with a **Theory of Meaning**. You might try wondering politely if Davidson's extension of Tarskian semantics is really viable: but on no account get drawn on the subject.

With a little practice, you can easily create your own meta-disciplines, and indeed not just disciplines: **G. E. L. Owen** used to refer to his 'meta-diary', which was the piece of paper on which he had written where he had left his diary. There is no doubt, however, that of the legitimate 'metas' metaphysics is the big one.

Metaphysics

Metaphysics is about what there *really* is (as opposed to merely what there is, which is of course ontology), what people in unguarded moments tend to refer to as the Underlying Structure of the world. Put like that, it sounds somewhat like contemporary particle physics, if less obviously dotty, and there is a sense in which traditional metaphysics has been taken over by modern science. Metaphysics is difficult; if the Positivists are right, it's impossible. It is in fact increasingly common to get to the end of a three-year University course without having the least idea of what it is. You, as a bluffer, need have only the vaguest of notions – but it is important, as always, to have strong opinions about it.

Whether there is a God, what is the nature of Substance, the Structure of Causal connections, whether British Rail exists on Sundays: all these might be said to be broadly metaphysical questions, which is to say, among other things, that they admit of no clear answers. This is what the **Logical Positivists**, an inter-war collection of Viennese philosophers with silly names, had against it.

When talking about, or (safer) simply mentioning, metaphysics, it is best to adopt one of two approaches. You can simply refuse to accept the existence of any such subject (best done with a patronising smile), in which case the **Positivists** come in handy; or alternatively, you can attempt to invest your remarks on the matter with the air of someone penetrating some ineffable mystery. The early Wittgenstein (*q.v.*) is ideal for the first purpose; the late one will do for the latter. Wittgenstein is always good value, for the excellent reason that, while almost everyone has heard of him, almost no-one has actually read him, and fewer still can claim with any conviction to have understood him.

With the Positivists, the best material comes from their Principle of Verifiability. This states that we know the meaning of any sentence only if we know what it would take for that sentence to be true. If there is no method of verifying it, at least in principle, then the sentence is meaningless. This approach has the devastating, and not unpleasing, effect of making almost all traditional metaphysics, as well as much of what is said by economists and Church of England clergymen, literally meaningless.

Ethics

One of the great pleasures of the philosopher's life is being able to tell everyone (and not just children and dogs) what they ought to do. This is Ethics. Speaking generally, and you will be, there are basically two types of Ethical Theory (the recently-fashionable Communitarianism and the so-called Ethics of Care, really amount to little more than saying its nice – and feminist, and un-patriarchal, and so on – to be nice to people: this hardly qualifies as a theory).

You can be either a **Consequentialist**, or a **Deontologist**. The former hold that an action's moral quality is determined solely by its results. The latter, on the other hand, hold that there are some things that one ought to do, and others that one should refrain from, irrespective of what the actual or probable results of that action are. The most famous version of consequentialism is Utilitarianism, classically articulated by **Bentham** and **Mill** in the last century, and still alive and kicking. The classical form of the Utilitarian ethic holds that one should act so as to produce the greatest good for the greatest number. How that good is defined, and by whom, what to do in the case of incompatible goods, whether the total number of people involved matters or not, and if so how, are only some of the initial problems with interpreting the doctrine.

The principal trouble with Utilitarianism, or rather any variety of it (it comes in a number of flavours), is that it gives rise in Problem-cases to 'counter-intuitive' results. Try out the following against someone who claims to be a Utilitarian. Suppose you have three people, each suffering from a terminal collapse of one of their vital organs, whereas you, on the other hand, are an offensively healthy animal. As a Utilitarian, you would have to consent to the idea of being hauled off to hospital, and being cut open to transplant your healthy organs into the bodies of your ailing friends, ensuring a net gain of two lives. Anti-utilitarians feel, not implausibly, that you might not be too happy to go along with this as an idea.

The advantage of Utilitarianism is that, at least in its basic idea, it is fairly straightforward, although it has been objected that if you take the idea of consequentialisms seriously, you would spend your whole time trying to calculate the precise effect of any action, and thus end up doing nothing at all. It is generally not a good idea to claim that this is in itself an advantage of the theory.

Deontologists, by contrast, are a good deal more troublesome. The obvious difficulty consists in spelling out just what the duties, and concomitant rights, actually are. There is very little consensus on this, and it gets us into the **Subjectivist/Objectivist** debate: are morals discovered, as the objectivist has it, by some peculiar faculty, or are they rather matters of convenience, created in a more or less arbitrary way in order to make social, and most forms of anti-social, activity possible? It's a good idea to have a view on this.

If you decide to take up subjectivism, you should be aware that it is likely to commit you, unless you contrive some pretty fancy footwork, to **Cultural Relativism**, a stance not without its dangers. A Cultural Relativist holds that no one society has the right to say what is right or wrong about any other one, which takes a good deal of fun out of life, as well as making international relations, as currently practised, by the Conservative Party, an impossibility. This entails that, while infanticide and infibulation may be a bit out of order in Guildford, they can be perfectly O.K. in New Guinea. This can get you into serious difficulties, particularly with feminists.

Perhaps the best line to take is that adopted by **Dick Hare**, who remarked that he'd never been able to understand what was supposed to be the difference between the two stances: and added, devastatingly, that he'd never met anyone else who could either. This is a brilliant example of one of the advanced bluffer's most useful techniques, to pretend that the blindingly obvious is in fact hopelessly obscure – it's just that lesser minds can't appreciate its inherent complexity. Wittgenstein employed this method from time to time, but Hare is the master. He once claimed that he didn't really understand the meaning of the word 'it'.

But whatever your thoughts on the origins of morals, you should have some stance on moral theory: which brings us back to Deontologies. For classical versions, Kant is the name to conjure with, and his famous Categorical Imperative. This has several different formulations in his work which is good news for the bluffer: "Yes, but which version of Kant's Principle did you have in mind?" has been known to work like a charm, but is perhaps most usually, if obscurely, expressed as follows:

'Act only according to that maxim by which you can at the same time will that it should become a general law.'

This is generally interpreted to mean that you should only do the sort of things you wouldn't mind everyone else doing. There are difficulties with this. You might quite like having a snooze but wouldn't much like the idea of the rest of the world joining you in the same bed.

The principal advocates of deontologies these days are the churches and some sections of the Conservative Party. Philosophers, who are for the most part, at least in their personal lives, an amoral bunch of rogues (this is particularly true of moral philosophers), tend to think less in terms of duties than of rights, and to create **Rights Theories**. You have a Right insofar as there is either something you deserve, or something you should be allowed to get away with.

An important principle of most Rights Theories is that of 'Universalisability' which is, because of its length, an excellent word to bandy around. It means that you or I have a right only if everyone else has a similar one. So, if you buy Rights Theory along with Universalisability, you have to be pretty careful about what rights you claim to have, in case some other clown gets his hands on them.

Nonetheless, rights are extremely good value. For a start, almost everybody who thinks they have rights at all holds inconsistent beliefs about them, (for instance, that everyone has the right to life, but also that the oppressed have a right to kill tyrants) and it usually only requires a little ingenuity to discover and exploit them. This will give you a great feeling of intellectual superiority, and leave your adversary nursing a strong, if morally prohibited, desire to tear your eyes out – which is, after all, what it's all about.

The drawback, of course, is that you yourself may be accused of holding an Inconsistent Set of principles. If this happens, you should say that the principles you have been trapped into admitting were not meant to be unqualified; in other words there are exceptions that prove the rule, whatever that means. In certain specifiable circumstances (try and avoid having to specify them), one will take precedence over another: your principal set, you will remark sagely, is hierarchised; and you might point out gravely that it's all a matter of systematising your moral science

Another useful technical distinction to draw is that between Act-centred and Agent-centred theories of ethics. As you might guess, this is all about whether what really matters in morals is what sort of thing we do, or what kind of people we are (for we all know that the most appalling social blights can on occasion do things we approve of, even solicitors). Of course, any sensible theory is neither exclusively one thing nor the other; and it's generally safe to say something to that effect without fear of having to say just how much of one, or the exact proportion of the other. Another useful gambit is: "Don't you think that presupposes an excessively act-centred (or agent-centred, as the case may be) view of morality?"

As a general rule, it is advisable to have a set of unorthodox (and infuriating) views, particularly on the so-called New Moral Problems, if indeed they're new at all. NMPs are difficulties generated by such advances as test-tube babies, surrogacy, foetal experimentation, and the like. The possibility of large-scale cloning is another, if potential, NMP.

Euthanasia, which has been practised in one form or

another since the emergence of the human race, is for some reason frequently considered a New Moral problem. Be suitably dismissive about this. There is a customary distinction between active and passive euthanasia. The former is actually killing, the latter merely letting die. Try arguing that this distinction is spurious. 'After all, the doctor who refuses treatment *intends* the patient to die; and he has the means to prolong life: so by his negligence he is just as responsible for the patient's death as if he took a meat-cleaver to him.' A subtle variation of this is to hold that passive euthanasia is actually *more* immoral than the active sort, which can after all be carried out in a humane and painless way; whereas with the former you effectively ensure that the patient dies in extreme pain. This argument is particularly effective with doctors – it enrages them, and the world holds few sweeter sights than the hopping-mad physician.

As for other moral problems, new, middle-aged, or positively ancient, our advice is to cut your cloth to suit the occasion. If confronting a feminist about abortion, or any question involving Foetal Rights, you might politely enquire if a Woman's Right to Choose extends to a Right to Choose to Kill. You need to be prepared for this, and have good reasons for thinking foetuses have rights; it isn't good enough to be a Catholic – Bentham's view that the ability to suffer pain confers rights may come in handy.

This is an area that rewards argumentative inventiveness. It is not without risks, but it can pay rich dividends. Find a moral position, fortify it with suitable arguments (they don't have to be *sound*, but it does help if they're *valid* – see Glossary for this important distinction), and you're away. After a while you will probably find that most of your friends are as well. For instance, you could argue that marriage is immoral. This is surprisingly easy, and delightfully irritating, particularly to newly-weds and their

37

parents – but we leave you to work out the details. Bluffing is a creative activity.

Logic

This is an important branch of philosophical enquiry. Logic, as a formal study, is fiendishly difficult, and best left well alone. All you need to know is that it was all right when everyone was doing Aristotelian Syllogistic (some people, including most Catholic philosophers, seem to be under the impression everyone still is); but it all got fouled up in the last century by the development of mathematical logic, in particular by **Gottlob Frege** (an excellent name to drop, even if he was – rather more than Nietzsche – an anti-semitic proto-fascist), **Russell** and **Whitehead** (*q.v.*). The new logic could do a lot more work (technically, it can deal with the logic of relations; relations between things, that is, not the thought-processes of your father-in-law), but is much harder.

Things got worse with the development of Alternative Logics sometimes entertainingly known as Deviant Logics. These increase the number of truth-values and question the validity of certain traditional logical laws, such as the Law of the Excluded Middle, which says (roughly) that everything either is something or it isn't. Under no circumstances commit yourself on this.

In addition to Formal Logic and of course meta-logic, there is **Philosophical Logic**. Like many things, this sounds better in an American accent: try it and see. This is a large and confusing area rather like Milton Keynes, and, also like Milton Keynes, it should be given a wide berth. You might like to know that one of its central concerns is Theory of Meaning but we rather doubt it. You might go as far as to comment sadly that none of the available Semantic Theories on the market seems very satisfactory, but on no account try to explain why. It is usually safe to adopt this line, as it is one of the pervasive features of philosophy that nothing in it is ever entirely satisfactory.

Epistemology

All you really need to know about epistemology is how to spell it. "But how can we know that we know that?" is effective at times, but mustn't be over-used. Epistemology nowadays is frequently done under the auspices of something called **Cognitive Science**, a hybrid of logic, linguistics, psychology, and computer science, which has to do with modelling reasoning, human as well as machine (Articifical Intelligence, or better AI) and (unsurprisingly in the case of the former at least) makes much use of Deviant Logics. It is also far too complicated for anything (except possibly an Artificial Intelligence) to understand.

Philosophy of Religion

Like most things in philosophy, this is very much better as a destructive than it is as a constructive pursuit. People with strong religious views are excellent meat for the good philosophical bluffer, in that, while they are usually sensitive and can be deeply hurt by what you say, they are almost invariably too polite to say so.

If you don't want to get embroiled in the issue of whether God exists, and if so, what He thinks He's playing at, the best area to steer conversation into is the

Problem of Evil: if God loves us and the world, why are we and it so unspeakably grotty?

An elegantly beautiful formal version of this argument was supplied by **Lactantius**:

> Given that there is evil (and bearing in mind the supposed attributes of God), then either:
> 1) God knows about it, cares about it, but can't do anything about it; or
> 2) He would care about it, could do something about it, but doesn't know about it, or
> 3) He knows about it, could do something about it but doesn't care about it.

Philosophy of Science

As philosophy is essentially a meta-activity, there can be philosophies of just about anything, and science is no exception. How do scientists develop theories? What is the relation between theory and evidence? What is the experimental method? How does one theory gain ascendancy over another without money changing hands? These, and similar questions, are the province of the Philosophy of Science. It has enjoyed a boom in the last fifty years or so, partly because it gives philosophers the unfamiliar sensation that what they are doing is of some relevance to something, and partly because it is yet another area in which they have the pleasure of telling people where they get off.

Karl Popper (a good name) figured prominently in the development of the debates, with his view that theories can never be verified (i.e. proved true); they can only be falsified (i.e. shown to be up the spout). The reason for this is that no amount of empirical evidence will ever show beyond all doubt that the world will continue to behave in the way it has always been observed to; whereas one bad result such as water boiling at twelve degrees, or an edible British Rail sandwich, can falsify an entire theory.

The reason for this, according to Popper, is that proper theories are made up of exceptionless generalisations universally-quantified, or, more intelligibly, they consist of sentences of the form 'All somethings are something else'. According to Popper, science progresses by means of Bold Conjectures ('The world is entirely made of cheese') followed by Conclusive Refutations ('It can't be: this bit won't spread on my biscuit').

The trouble with this as a view is that, generally speaking, the bolder the conjecture, the more obviously dotty it is. Various people have offered different accounts: a good name to drop is that of **T.S. Kuhn** who prefers to talk of Scientific Revolutions which involve what he calls Paradigm Shifts. This idea is extraordinarily difficult to pin down, and for that reason invaluable. Broadly, it means that people just decide to stop looking at the world in one way, and start looking at it in another. More devastating for Popper was the remark of **Hilary Putnam**, that if Popper was right, no theory is falsifiable either, for no theory, just like no man, is an island. They always involve Auxiliary Assumptions about the nature of the universe, and faced with an Anomaly, you have a choice: chuck out either the theory, or an Auxiliary Assumption, or both, if you're feeling extravagant.

Putnam is, incidentally, perhaps the most distinguished contemporary Amercian philosopher. He is useful to the bluffer because of his engaging habit of completing changing his extremely subtle and complex views on thing just as other philosophers are beginning to think that they understand them – about once every ten years or so – outdoing even Wittgenstein. You may thus confidently prefix any claim with the words "as Putnam says", secure in the knowledge that somewhere, and at some time, he will have done.

Other names to drop are **Imre Lakatos** if you can pronounce it, and **Paul Feyerabend**, a self-confessed methodological anarchist, who urges that scientists adopt as their research motto the maxim 'anything goes'. In addition to his having imported Cole Porter into philosophy, something no-one else has ever managed to do, Feyerabend is a notable eccentric: he used to end his lectures at the London School of Economics by leaping out of an open (fortunately ground-floor) window, on to a powerful motorbike, and riding noisily away.

THE CONTEMPORARY SCENE

The Anglo-Saxon Philosophers

Anglo-Saxon philosophers (including the Finns, of course) tend to deny that they are part of any particular school or sect: indeed they are liable to regard philosophical sectarianism as a dangerous Continental habit, and consequently one to be despised. Nonetheless, they do tend to stick together, as if seeking safety in numbers and perhaps believing, possibly correctly, that they need it. They are invariably lumped together as 'Analytic Philosophers', even if they've never actually analysed anything.

Before the First World War, the two most important

figures in British philosophy were probably (remember, don't commit yourself, if you can avoid it) **Bertrand Russell** and **G. E. Moore**. Russell made his reputation with the publication of *Principia Mathematica*, co-written with **A. N. Whitehead**, and consequently sometimes referred to as 'Russell and Whitehead', in the manner of authoritative books on sex. This is an extremely detailed exposition of formal symbolic logic, and as such, not to be recommended as reading for long train journeys, indeed, not to be recommended as reading at all.

Moore, not to be outdone as far as portentous-sounding Latinate titles were concerned, reacted by producing his *Principia Ethica,* an influential treatise on moral philosophy, in which he held that 'good' was indefinable, but was the name of a non-natural quality. A conception of Moore's much discussed in this context is that of the 'Naturalistic Fallacy'. It is, however, rather difficult to say exactly what this is: Moore's idea seems to be that you can't define ethical terms in terms of non-ethical ones, and you can't deduce ethical propositions from factual, non-ethical ones.

This confusion makes the Naturalistic Fallacy extremely useful, particularly if you follow Moore himself, and never argue why it is a fallacy, but simply assert that it is one. You can supplement this in conversation usefully with another concept of Moore's, the Open Question Argument. This asserts that no matter what factually holds of some particular object or property (that people like it, for instance; or that it is cheese-flavoured), it is still an Open Question whether or not it is good. Moore was renowned for his robust no-nonsense approach to philosophy: he once informed an astonished lecture-hall that nothing was more certain than the fact he had two hands. It is not clear who had been disposed to doubt it.

As for Russell, his other major contributions to philosophy, (as opposed to his other major concerns which included pacifism and promiscuity, and may thus be summed up by the sixties slogan 'Make Love Not War' which Russell did into an enviably old age) include the discovery of Russell's Paradox with which he put paid to something rather disparagingly known as naïve set-theory, and the Theory of Descriptions. The Theory of Descriptions is an attempt to analyse the logic of natural language (remember this phrase), and in particular the problem of Proper Names. This, like most philosophical problems, isn't a problem to anyone who isn't a philosopher. Russell employed as examples regularly-used sentences of English such as "The present King of France is bald' or 'Scott wrote the Waverley novels'. The latter according to Russell actually means 'someone wrote the Waverley novels: only one person wrote the Waverley novels; and if anyone wrote the Waverley novels, that person was Scott'. From this one might be tempted to deduce that philosophers know as much about ordinary language as they do about ordinary people (see Introduction).

The proper attitude to Russell's *History of Western Philosophy* is to praise its style, lucidity and humour, while having reservations about its actual content: "A marvellous read, of course, but a bit tendentious, don't you think?" 'Don't you think?' is a rhetorical question, and should never be taken literally.

Perhaps the most influential philosophical meeting before the First World War occurred in 1912, when the (Very) Early **Wittgenstein** met Russell in Cambridge, and asked him (Russell) if he (the Very Early Wittgenstein) was a complete idiot: because if he was, he was going to become an aeroplane pilot. Russell told him to go away and write something; the Very Early

Wittgenstein did so, Russell read one line of it and told him he was far too clever to be an aviator.

The war interrupted the Very Early Wittgenstein's career in Cambridge, but he returned after it as the Early Wittgenstein, and proceeded to dominate philosophical life in Cambridge, and elsewhere, for the next thirty years. A charmingly eccentric figure, with a passion for dreadful films, he lived in a deck-chair under an electric fan in an otherwise entirely bare room in Trinity College. He published only one book in his lifetime, the *Tractatus Logico-Philosophicus*, in which he tackled such problems as the structure of the proposition, how language is meaningful, and the notions of truth and falsity.

His researches led him to the belief that only propositions built up out of basic atomic propositions with logical connectives were meaningful. Hence the name 'Logical Atomism' for this type of philosophy. Everything else was literally meaningless, and this gets rid of metaphysics, along with a lot of other things. Indeed, it has the unfortunate consequence of making almost all of the *Tractatus* itself, if true, meaningless.

The Early Wittgenstein acknowledged this, saying that only if in some sense you already knew what he meant, would you be able to understand his writing; and that his philosophy was like a ladder which you threw away after climbing it. Many people took this metaphor literally. The last sentence of the book sums it up: 'Whereof one cannot speak, thereof there must be silence' or, for the really ambitious bluffer: 'Wovon man nicht sprechen kann, darüber muß man schweigen.'

He then gave up philosophy for a period, thinking that he had said it all. However, he later changed his mind: this is the crucial point at which the Early Wittgenstein becomes the Later Wittgenstein, and as such the second truly influential figure in philosophy between the wars (after the

Early Wittgenstein).

In the *Tractatus*, Wittgenstein had thought that propositions had meaning because they were like pictures of the facts they referred to. The Later Wittgenstein disagreed with him, assimilating meaning to use, and allowing that ordinary language was both more complex (and more meaningful) than the Early Wittgenstein had given it credit for. The posthumous result of this is the *Philosophical Investigations*. He died in 1951; ever since when, there has been a steady stream of posthumously-published note-books, records of lectures, laundry lists, notes to his landlady, etc., giving him the remarkable distinction of having written only one book during his lifetime but about fifteen after his death. And the stream shows no sign of abating.

After the War, English philosophy centred on Oxford, although Cambridge would disagree, when a mysterious entity known as 'Oxford Philosophy' or more derisively 'linguistic philosophy' came into existence. Its chief exponents were **Gilbert Ryle**, a renowned pipe-smoker and **J. L. Austin**, another renowned pipe-smoker. Austin was well-known for his 'Saturday mornings' at which a group of distinguished philosophers, distinguished principally by the fact that they all smoked pipes, would get together to discuss the subtle nuances of ordinary language, or splitting hairs, depending on your point of view. This tended to take the form of distinguishing six different meanings of words like 'wheelbarrow', and not surprisingly provoked anger or derision among those who were excluded for whatever reason, such as not being clever enough, or not smoking a pipe.

However, it is generally accepted, except of course in Oxford, that since the War the centre of gravity of Anglo-Saxon philosophy has shifted to North America (even the Finnish bit), a state of affairs which may not be totally unrelated to the fact that American universities pay enormous salaries. The Grand Old Man of American philosophy is **Willard van Orman Quine** ('Van' to his mates), who is memorable for holding that Kant's distinction between analytic and synthetic (see Glossary) is at best vague and at worst useless, and for having called a book of his *From a Logical Point of View* after a Harry Belafonte calypso.

His successors include **Saul Kripke** in the field of philosophical logic and the study of Modality (don't worry about what that is), whose major work, *Naming and Necessity*, which is about Proper Names, Sense and Reference, Possible Worlds, and many other terms you will find at the end of the book, is worth mentioning in passing as perhaps the most significant piece of philosophical work done since the War.

You will also have noticed how in American philosophy the Silly Name is as great a help as it was to the Viennese Positivists: many of whom ended up in America, perhaps for this reason – an impression confirmed by **Alvin Plantinga**, a modal logician and a philosopher of religion (a slightly unstable combination), and **Robert Nozick** a radical right-wing political anarchist, who thinks that everything should be privatised.

One American philosopher of importance is **John Rawls**, whose major book, *A Theory of Justice*, has been widely bought. Basically, Rawls holds that justice can be analysed into two principles:

1. That everyone should have the same freedom as everyone else, and, given that constraint, as much freedom as possible;

2. That economic inequalities between people are only justified if the worst off are in fact better off under this arrangement than they would be under any more equal one.

Be careful with this: it isn't as silly as it seems at first sight, but it does allow for extreme inequalities of goods, which may be held to count against the system – unless of course you happen to benefit from them. This type of thing is known as a Theory of Distributive Justice, and can come in handy.

The Continentals

The Continentals come in two main varieties, the French and the Germans.

Perhaps the most important Continental philosophical movement of recent times has been **Existentialism** which has had both French and German adherents. The principal French exponent was **Sartre**, an enviable polymath, who combined philosophy with active Marxist politics, the writing of novels and plays, and a prodigious capacity for alcohol. He coined the slogan 'existence precedes essence', which means, broadly, that we should be less concerned with what *type* of things things are than with the fact *that* they are.

Existentialists resist classifications, tending to insist on the autonomy of the individual: thus, they tend to get rather miffed about being called Existentialists at all. Existentialism, at least the French variety of it, has strong literary connections, Camus and Sartre himself being the most important exponents. The literature tends to concentrate on the concept of the *acte gratuit* or gratuitous action (refer to it French, of course), which is supposed to be the essence of the Existentialist's affirmation of his own existence. To the uncommitted, it generally seems more like a piece of bloody-minded capriciousness. As the *acte gratuit*, at least in literature, tends to be of a violent, or at the very least an anti-social, nature, life with an

Existentialist (at least a French one) must be a bit nerve-racking.

The Germans, among whom names to drop are **Martin Heidegger** and **Karl Jaspers**, are a rather different bunch. They have no pretensions to literary excellence, luckily, and tend to be more explicit about their debt to earlier philosophers such as **Kierkegaard** and **Edmund Husserl**, a turn of the century German who developed in a systematic and thoroughly Teutonic way the concept of Phenomenology, i.e. the attempt to penetrate below the surface of the appearances of things to the basic reality of our conscious apprehension of them (or something).

Existentialism carries no religious commitment one way or the other: Sartre was an atheist, Jaspers a Christian; Heidegger was a Nazi, but this is generally conveniently forgotten. An interesting point to note is that, whereas books of philosophy written in English generally have to have three elements to their titles *Language, Truth and Logic; Truth, Probability and Paradox; Mind, Language and Reality*, being some prominent examples, the requisite number for Existentialist titles seems to be two, as in Heidegger's *Sein und Zeit – Being and Time*; or Sartre's *L'Etre et le Neant – Being and Nothingness*. Anglo-Saxon analytic philosophers are inclined to despise Existentialism for not being sufficiently analytic: Existentialists are inclined to despise Anglo-Saxon analytic philosophers for simply not being sufficiently.

Enough has been said elsewhere in this book about **Logical Positivism**, and in any case its exponents are really more closely linked with the Anglo-Saxon tradition; many of them fled Europe and Hitler in the thirties for America, where **Rudolph Carnap** and **Carl Hempel** have been particularly influential since the War, particularly in the philosophy of science. The most

49

important of the English Logical Positivists (which, incidentally, include the Early, but not the Late, Wittgenstein) was **A. J. Ayer** (always refer to him as 'Freddie'), who is still best known for his first book, *Language, Truth and Logic*, although he later came to believe that it was wrong from beginning to end, which must have been rather galling. Ayer was also influenced by Russell, not least in the conduct of his shambolic personal life.

One major element of Continental thought remains to be discussed: **Structuralism**, and its rather shadowy successor **Post-Structuralism**, which itself seems to have become the positively opaque **Post-Modernism**.

Structuralism originally began as a method in Linguistics with **Saussure**, and penetrated Anthropology with **Lévi-Strauss**, since when it hasn't looked back, at least in France and the English Literature departments of American Universities. Almost no-one will nowadays admit to being a Structuralist, and it is quite hard to say what exactly Structuralists are. It is however, important to have strong views about them. They are almost universally ignored in British philosophy departments which demonstrates the rigorous analytic preoccupations of British philosophy, or its appalling insularity, depending on which side you're on. Make sure you're on one, but only one. Characteristic of Structuralism and Post-Structuralism is its distrust of academic disciplines, and its impenetrable jargon.

Leading exponents include: **Roland Barthes** (in the field of literary criticism and its social ramifications), **Michel Foucault** (history, sociology, and, finally, sex) and **Jacques Derrida** (language, literary criticism, rhetoric). The latter is in many ways the most interesting, if also the most infuriatingly obscure. Opinions vary widely as to his stature as a thinker: genius or charlatan, according to taste. He has particularly annoyed analytical philosophers (Anglo-Saxon ones, that is), at least those who've been bothered to read any of his stuff, by his attempts to show that beneath its carefully cultivated surface of rigour, logic, analysis, and dispassionate enquiry, analytic philosophy is a highly tendentious, rhetorical, subjective business.

This he does by employing a method known as Deconstructionism, now a major American industry. Essentially it consists of showing that any literary work necessarily generates within itself fatal contradictions thus undermining the argument it ostensibly advances.

Note that deconstruction in fact deconstructs itself (rather like Wittgenstein's *Tractatus*), a fact which the deconstructionists themselves seem not to care about (much to analytic philosophers' fury: this can be a technique worth copying).

The great advantage of Post-Modernism is that nobody, including its exponents, has any idea what it is. Saying of something (anything, in fact) that it is 'Post-Modern' is a useful gambit much deployed by its leading practitioners, including **Deleuze** and **Baudrillard**.

Perhaps the safest courses to take with Continental Philosophy in general are either:

a) to claim that what is said is literally meaningless;
b) to say, derisively, that whatever it is, it isn't philosophy (the Analytic line);
c) to remark cautiously that it shouldn't be dismissed out of hand. (This is best done to someone advancing one of the other two views.)

SOME USEFUL TECHNIQUES

In this section, we offer a brief guide to some of the more important basic arts of the philosophical bluffer: others can be inferred from the rest of the text.

1. The Question
It is always a good idea to couch your remarks in the form of a question, particularly if you've no idea what you're talking about, as happens about 85 per cent of the time in philosophy. Thus, you should prefer "Don't you think that presupposes some rather implausible assumptions?" to "That presupposes some implausible assumptions".

2. The Hedge
Never commit yourself: if it's possible to hedge, and it nearly always is in philosophy, then hedge. Leave yourself routes of escape. An incidental advantage of this procedure is to confer upon the bluffer an air of proper intellectual caution. Clauses like "It seems to me at least" (when it doesn't), or "I'm inclined to think that" (even when you aren't), and "Perhaps there's something to be said for it" (particularly when there plainly isn't) are to be cultivated. The really expert philosophical bluffer will never say anything that he or she can't quietly and unobtrusively retract if the need arises. In this respect they closely resemble the professional philosopher.

3. Delivery
It is important to make your contributions in the right tone of voice; this should be slow, measured and considered. Try and give the impression that everything you say has been carefully thought out: you will find that the most blatant drivel can be made to sound both intelligent and profound.

4. Appearance

Many otherwise competent bluffers lose valuable kudos for not paying sufficient attention to this. Broadly speaking, there are two types of philosopher:

1) The precise, neat, impeccably-dressed Nietzschian Superman;
2) The unbelievably scruffy, messy, absent-minded Human Wreck.

The latter is perhaps the more common, but the former is by no means unknown, and a suave, cool, controlled manner can pay rich dividends; while on the other hand the Magnus Pyke type of extraordinary eccentricity is surprisingly difficult to carry off. So, other things being equal, we would recommend (1), unless you suffer from some crippling personal disqualification, such as the physique of Quasimodo allied to the dress-sense of Michael Foot. (1) is particularly to be recommended for women: it gets them a better hearing.

5. Itemisation

Philosophy is supposed to be an orderly, clear-headed activity, treating confusing and difficult matters in a logical, rigorous, lucid fashion (no really, it is). The truly great bluffer is the one who can give the impression of doing this while in fact doing exactly the opposite; and an aid to this end is itemisation. "That seems to me to raise at least three questions" is a good start, especially if it doesn't raise any at all. The more questions you can raise the better. In general, go for high stakes: three is a minimum, four adequate, and six or even seven questions have been known to wreak devastating destruction. Trust to luck and ingenuity to come up with them as you go along. In any case if there are enough of them, your adversary will lose count.

6. Props
We are now getting to the advanced stage, and most higher-level enthusiasts cultivate at least one prop. For men the most effective and versatile is the pipe. Many genuine philosophers smoke pipes. The reason is probably self-evident: if you are asked a really awkward question, or are otherwise put on the spot, all you have to do is take the pipe out of an inside pocket (you will find that this makes the inside pocket particularly disgusting after a few days: but bluffers must suffer for their art, like everyone else), after making some preliminary remark such as: "Well, the really important thing about that seems to me at least to be", and set about lighting it. You can make this operation last five minutes with no difficulty, and much longer with practice, and provided you interject the occasional comment of an entirely non-committal nature as you knock, clean, scrape, blow through, dismantle, re-assemble, load, pack, tamp, light, draw on, re-light, re-tamp, draw on again, and emit large and noxious clouds of smoke from the pipe, no-one will suspect that you're playing for time. Do this well enough, and you can avoid having to answer the question at all.

Other props and social ticks, like offering cigarettes, cleaning glasses, blowing the nose powerfully and lengthily, or even feigning a fit of coughing all have their uses, but none of them beats the pipe, which also manages for some reason to make whoever is smoking it look knowledgeable.

7. Language
Select a few pieces of jargon you like the sound of; then flog them to death. And remember the Golden Rule: never say anything in English if you can say it in some other language (preferably German).

8. Playing for Time

It is never out of order to remark, with an air of deep seriousness, that you will have to give the matter more thought. This is again a doubly effective technique, in that it both does away with the obligation to say anything that might commit you to something, and also in that it tends to make your adversary feel intellectually inferior. This latter is particularly true if the matter in question is in fact something blindingly obvious. Remember: always strive to complicate the essentially simple.

9. Pretence of Profundity

This is closely related, of course (note that 'of course': properly deployed, a weapon of devastating conversational power), to the previous technique: "It really is much more difficult than most people give it credit for" is a great phrase to use in a crisis.

10. Invention

If you're ever in a tight spot, with no possible avenue of escape, don't underestimate the power of sheer invention. Descartes once remarked that there is no position or doctrine so absurd that it hasn't at some time been held by some philosopher or other. Using this as your cue, feel free to invent philosophers at will. Ideal for this purpose are little-known 19th century German metaphysicians. You could make use of Heinrich Niemand, Professor of the Philosophy of Dairy Produce at the University of Bad Homburg, a wonderful man, who, in addition to having the virtue of never actually existing, gets one out of all kinds of difficulties. "Well, it may be daft, but Niemand said it" you say on these occasions, and it generally works like a dream.

What Philosophy Isn't

A common misconception is that philosophy is something like religion really. A good line to take in the face of this is to observe that philosophy is concerned with the undermining and questioning of dogmas, whereas religion is all about accepting and supporting them.

You will also meet people (if you're not careful) who claim to be interested in something called 'Eastern Philosophy', or 'Oriental Mysticism'. There is only one thing to do when confronted by this sort of person: point out firmly that whatever Eastern Philosophy, or Oriental Mysticism, is, it isn't philosophy. Be firm about this. This is not to underestimate the practitioners of this arcane art: some people do quite nicely out of it, and there is mileage in mysticism.

Footnote: How to Be a Mystic

1. Invent a few meaningless paradoxes (such as 'the only true light is in the darkness', or 'each step forwards is a step backwards').
2. Have a line in pointless proverbs (like 'he who talks with the goldfish is to lucky to receive an answer', or 'the taller the tree, the thinner the fruit').
3. Profess a belief in at least one palpable meta-physical absurdity, such as that Everything is All One, or that Ordinary Reality is merely a Base Illusion in Comparison with the True Light of the Godhead. Remember to talk in Capital Letters.
4. Intimate in an obscure way that the Road to Enlightenment, though Long and Hard, is Ultimately Traversable; and hint that a good method of traversing it is by entering on a Close Physical Relationship with yourself.
5. At all times wear a Benign Smile, for practical purposes indistinguishable from the Inane Grin.

GLOSSARY

Remember the Bluffer's Golden Rule: things always sound better in languages people can't understand. This is particularly true for some reason, of German. Thus:

Zeitgeist – The Spirit of the Age, the general prevailing viewpoint of mankind at any particular time (if any).

Weltanschauung (a really good one, this) – View of the World; World-picture. Experiment with remarks like "it's the kind of thing that forces one to change one's Weltanschauung".

Erkenntis – Knowledge; also the name of the journal of the Viennese Logical Positivists (men like Otto Neurath, Carl Hempel and Rudolph Carnap), who were known as:

Der Wiener Kreis – The Vienna Circle.

Sinn und Bedeutung – Sense and Reference: a distinction between two sorts of signification made by Frege, and one of the corner-stones of modern philosophical logic.

Gesamtheit – Totality: useful in Wittgenstein's dictum: 'Die Welt ist die Gesamtheit der Tatsachen, nicht der Dinge' (the world is the totality of facts, not things). Not to be confused with 'Gesundheit'.

But you can't get away with German all the time. You must have some grip (however tenuous) on the technical vocabulary in English.

Logic – A very useful word. It can designate either a formal system of reasoning (like Aristotelian Syllogistic), or can be used more loosely to indicate the argumentative force of a piece of reasoning. "What is the logic of that argument?" is a useful question to ask, particularly if you need time to get out of a tight corner.

An **Argument**, which in philosophical parlance is a reasoned exposition of a point of view, not, as in ordinary language, a blazing row (though it is surprising how often one degenerates into the other) can be either valid or invalid, sound or unsound. An argument is valid if it consists of premises linked in such a way that, if they are true, then the conclusion drawn for them is true. It is sound only if all the premises are true and it is valid as well (thus ensuring the truth of the conclusion).

Consistency is a great weapon in the bluffer's armoury. Two or more propositions are inconsistent if it is impossible for them all to be true at the same time. You can never point out other people's inconsistencies too frequently. Try and avoid having them point out yours.

Propositions are simply sentences that are either true or false, like "President Clinton is a hamster"; thus, on this definition, "Would you like to come back to my place and see my collection of antique French cheeses?" is, oddly enough, not a proposition. **Atomic propositions** are basic propositions that assert something about something else, and as such were thought by the earlier Wittgenstein (though not of course by the later Wittgenstein) to be the fundamentals of language.

Entailment — The relation between the **premises** of a **sound** or **valid** argument and its **conclusion**: if x entails y, then y follows from x (it is more impressive to talk of entailment than of one thing following from another).

Conditionals – Propositions of the form 'if...then...' they are the basic building-blocks of logical argument.

Counterfactuals – A type of conditional in which the first bit (the 'if' clause) is false, such as: 'if pigs had wings, then the police-car would be obsolete'. They are interesting to the philosopher because it is very difficult to analyse their **truth-conditions**; and handy for the bluffer in such remarks as "I'm not sure how to interpret that counterfactua". They are sometimes known as 'subjunctive conditionals', generally by people who want you to know they've done Latin.

Truth-Conditions – The conditions under which something is true; an awful lot of fuss is made about them, considering.

Triviality – Not, as might perhaps be expected, a general characterisation of the whole philosophical enterprise, but a logical concept. Something is **trivially true** if its truth follows without any special logical inference from something else: thus, if both 'p' and 'q' are true, trivially 'p' is true. It is surprising how much you can annoy quite equable people with remarks like "That's true; but of course it's only trivially true".

Rational – (1) reasoned; (2) (*Math.*) a number that can be expressed as a function of two other numbers; (3) anything you yourself say.

Irrational – (1) unreasoned; (2) (*Math.*) a number that can't be expressed as a function of two other numbers; (3) anything anyone else says.

Analytic and Synthetic – A useful distinction of Kant's between two types of truth: **analytic truths** are those which are true solely in virtue of the meanings of the words they contain independently of the state of the word (like 'all bachelors are unmarried'); **synthetic truths** on the other hand (like 'no haddock is an opera-singer'), are true or false according to empirical circumstances (there *might* have been haddocks who performed at La Scala). It is one of the great tragedies of life that analytic truths, though certain and indubitable, are of very little use, while synthetic truths, though of use, are by no means certain or indubitable. Kant actually disagreed with this, thinking that there could be *a priori* (see below) synthetic truths, such as those of geometry. But he was wrong, unfortunately.

A priori and a posteriori – A similar type of distinction. A priori truths can be known independently of any empirical facts; a posteriori ones cannot.

Necessary and Contingent – **Necessary** truths are those which could not possibly be otherwise; **contingent** ones are not. Thus "John Major is Prime Minister" is contingently true, whereas "John Major is John Major" is necessarily true (which shows there can be unfortunate necessary truths). Another way of putting this, much employed by the Americans, is to say that necessary truths are true in all Possible Worlds.

Possible Worlds – The whimsical creation of fanciful philosophers like **Liebniz**: a **Possible World** is any total state of affairs that might obtain (but, unluckily, generally doesn't). Realists (see below) about possible worlds, pre-eminently **David Lewis**, hold that infinitely many possible worlds really exist, and are no less real (although, confusingly, less *actual*) than this one. This has the comforting consquence that there are perfectly real (if unfortunately non-actual) worlds in which you are devastatingly good-looking, rich, and so on.

Idealism, as a philosophical concept, doesn't mean a concern with the welfare of baby seals (or indeed with the welfare of prominent French actresses concerned with the welfare of baby seals) or a belief in the Brotherhood of Man, but is rather the notion pioneered by Berkeley that external objects have no real existence distinct from their being perceived. Actually, Idealists have a great deal of difficulty explaining what exactly they mean by this, for they tend to maintain that this doesn't mean that objects are illusory; but it also seems that the thesis they are maintaining is an ontological rather than an epistemological one. Idealism is contrasted with:

Realism which is the belief that external objects really are there after all, and not just when someone is taking some notice of them. Realism, however, is a multiply ambiguous term in philosophy. In Philosophy of Science it is the view that scientific laws point to real relations in the physical world, and is contrasted with **Instrumentalism**: the view that scientific laws are merely predictive models. Putnam has recently invented something he calls 'internal realism', in which

61

there is no 'ready-made world' (a useful phrase), and yet things are not for all that irremediably subjective (which is exactly having your cake and eating it). This, he claims, is Kantian in inspiration, and perhaps for that reason difficult (if not impossible) to make head or tail of; and (also for that reason) ideal for the bluffer.

Nominalism – The position that **Universals** (sometimes also known as **Sortals**: broadly speaking, general terms like 'cat' and 'table'), don't have an independent existence apart from the collection of their instances, apart that is from the actual cats and tables which are parts of the furniture of the world. **Realists** in this sense believe that there are individual Universal entities which account for our being able to sort the world into coherent groupings of things. Plato was a realist in this sense (if in few others).

Semantics – A useful distinction to be aware of, particularly when talking to computer buffs, is that between Semantics and Syntax (or Syntactics). You supply a **Semantics** for an argument (or whatever) when you provide a method of translating the symbols it contains into something meaningful: to give a semantics for a language either pre-supposes or involves a **Theory of Meaning**. By contrast, the **Syntax** is simply the formal grammar of the system: whether the symbols are joined together properly or not. Thus you can follow the **Syntax** of a system without having the least idea of its **Semantics**. In fact, this is largely what the bluffer is doing in philosophy: he knows, ideally, how to manipulate the terms of the language, as the later (but not, of course the earlier) Wittgenstein might have put it; but he hasn't got the foggiest what it's really all about.

THE AUTHOR

Born in Lagos in 1957 for tax reasons, Jim Hankinson gave evidence at an early age of a naturally enquiring turn of mind, that propensity for asking questions (many of them highly impertinent) which led many observers to predict a career in philosophy, and several others to predict an early death. At school he was widely held to be too clever by half; but these days, by dint of persistent intake of alcohol he is only too clever by about ten per cent.

His undergraduate years were spent at Balliol College, Oxford, where he learned just how difficult Effortless Superiority can be, and what a full-time job is the cultivation of idleness and degeneracy.

Having acquired, to everyone's intense surprise, a First Class degree, he spent a period as a full-time sunbather in Crete before writing a doctoral thesis at King's College, Cambridge, on an area of philosophy so obscure that no-one could effectively examine him on it. On the strength of this he has taught (for a weak sense of 'teach') philosophy in Britain, Canada and the United States, always taking care to keep one step ahead of the tax authorities.

A believer in the value of rigorous discipline and self-motivation, he makes a point of working at least five minutes every day (including Wednesdays). His other interests, pressure of work permitting, include European Cinema, beer-brewing, and the development of increasingly complex and improbable fantasies involving Catherine Deneuve.

THE BLUFFER'S GUIDES®

Available at £1.99 and *£2.50 each:

All these books are available at your local bookshop or newsagent, or by post or telephone from: B.B.C.S., P.O.Box 941, Hull HU1 3VQ.

UK (& BFPO) Orders: £1.00 for the first book & 50p for each additional book up to a maximum of £2.50; Overseas (& Eire) Orders: £2.00 for the first book, £1.00 for the second & 50p for each additional book.

(24 hour Telephone Credit Card Line: 01482 224626).